IMAGINATIONPRESS

Moses'
GOSPEL
SONGS
of Nobility

TROY MOSES

Any references to historical events, real people, or real places are used fictitiously. Names, characters, and places are products of the author's imagination.

Front cover and Layout
by Francis Adams.

Printed by Lulu.com, in the United States of America.

ISBN 978-0-9995209-5-6

First printing edition 2018.

IMAGINATION PRESS LLC
101 Cherry Lane
Glen Burnie, Maryland 21060
USA
Phone: (301) 379-2709
Fax: (410) 636-0623

email: info@imaginationpressonline.com
www.imaginationpressonline.com

INTRODUCTION
From Mr. Tony Moses

It would be remiss of me if I first did not give praise to our Great God and honor is due to all those who are striving and toiling to bring their will in tune with the will of our Great and Mighty GOD.

Praise the Lord Saints, and I hope the lyrics of my gospel songs will be beneficial and inspiring to you all. Surely the words from my mouth and the thoughts that are poured out of my mind and into heart. I pray to God that he direct and lead your life, and that he speaks to you through me. I only put forth efforts to do as that which the Lord wishes to accomplish; God's way is the right way and the only way and without Him we are lost souls.

I praise God for the life, wisdom, knowledge, and understanding that I possess. Surely, life has only to offer what it puts in us. One who fails to plan, plans to fail. I recall reading that prosperity is not to be measured by wealth or worldly things, for being focused only on worldly things will pass away. The highest success is the health of mind and spirit, and we all must strive and toil to obtain. I acknowledge that no one has true success unless one has God in their life.

As for myself, I have been physically and sexually abused as a youth with no counseling. I pursued the calling of the streets with drugs and alcohol to escape my reality. I tried to cope with the pain, but I couldn't, and I turned on society and began committing crimes to support my addiction. Ignorant as I was then, I thought that I could cope, but the reality is that I never turned to God for assistance. I really needed a better understanding of myself, and some comfort and peace.

Well, to make a long story short, I finally gave my life over to God. It was in that year of 2008 when I finally left drugs, alcohol, and cigarettes. These items released the grip that I had on my mind mentally, and I said to myself, 'It's time to change". With the extra inspiration from God, I have been clean for 18 years. I am now 53 years old and I live to assist others who are still suffering with the disease of addiction. When I look to God, I know that I will be alright, and I know that I won't relapse. My response is "My Faith in God lets me know that I won't relapse."

We are God's creations and we all walk our own path in life of our own free will that God has given us. It is s in our nature; i.e. our in born tendencies that drives and urges us to be inconsistent at times. Therefore, I have established morals and principles to guard myself at times. I want to be   the strength of God made manifest and be the message that I bring, However, I had to first purify myself; i.e., my thoughts, words and deeds to enable me to be the strength of God made manifest and take my rightful place in the affairs of humanity.

In conclusion, I would like to say, I thank you all for your support and may God continue blessing you all as we continue to bring out the best that is already within us.

Peace & Love,
Your Brother & Friend In Christ,
Author Troy Moses
Written June 2, 2011.

Introduction
A poem Called:
Reminisce'

I often reminisce about my life;
On how I wish I was upright.
I often reminisce about my past;
On how I wish I would have completed my tasks;
I often reminisce on the negative things I have done;
Thinking I was slick, bad and cool;
When I was really young and dumb.
I often reminisce on how my life could have been;
Me having morals and principles and not living in sin.

I often reminisce on the positive of life I could have created:
Tomorrow isn't a promise to anyone, so right now I'm living it's not too late.

I often reminisce how my life would have turned out,
I know right one day at a time is all we got
Oh yes, I often reminisce of the past,
But now I have a spiritual –positive mind;
As I realize the present moment is the most valuable in time.

Oh yes, I reminisce mostly every day;
I acknowledge, I can't mostly every day;
I acknowledge, I can't mend my faults,
But I can amend my ways.
I reminisce!

May 19, 2010
Toy Moses

CONTENTS

I AM A Living Testimony

Chorus

Lead - Well, I want you all to know that I am a living testimony for God has transformed me, you see.

Chorus – He has made me free and I praise Jesus for paying my penalties.

Lead – He was unique, do you agree. Well I am a living testimony and from my actions you can all see indeed.

Chorus – He's now in tune with His divinity.

Lead – You see

Lead 1

Such a transformation spring forth cultivation/my dedication came about from my declaration/preparation a must/salvation a cost/Lost, oh no, need I testify/ He sacrifice and forever they thought He died/Arise, alive deep down inside/they tried to lie, but Divine Truth cannot hide/ Now I'm on a divine mission /and unto God belongs my tradition/

Chorus –Lead II

Now I can do the works of my Father/ I know God is please when we can help one another/ Propagate the Faith. I must say/ I'm a living witness each and every day/ For the word of God has really save me/ it's a blessing to know on what He gave me/ In His image and likeness He enslave me/ All Honor to those who show bravery/ uplift me from my addiction/ unto God's word we need to pay attention

Chorus – Lead III

I'm a living testimony and I am for real/ I'm walking in the path of Jesus indeed, I can heal/ Did He not say, "what I can do we can all pursue"/ bless with a will and the word of God, so don't misuse/ If you refuse to use what's on the menu/ the wrath of God will surely come down on you/ I tell you all if you're not ready/ I suggest you all go study/ So take heed to the word of God and live by/ so when your physical death come about on the Judgement Day you will rise/

Being Born Again

Chorus
Being born again, it's time to repent
Being born again, it's time to represent.
Being born again, do you know why He was sent,
Being born again, it's time to comprehend;
So listen up girls, boys, women and men.

Lead I
Being born again is a spiritual rebirth/ cleansing within and digging out all that dirt/ The Holy Spirit was sent into this world/ to carry out this new birth haven't you heard/ Transformation it's call for preparation/ it's time to prepare for our eternal destination/ Cultivation that's right such a process/ when knowing we don't suppose to get caught up in this body flesh/ For a time will come death/ and bring Spiritual minded means life, peace, and health/ Come on!

Lead II
What's of the flesh, I tell you will pass/ and what's of the spirit I tell you will last/ Such a task with no mask now can you grab/ let's take a journey into the lab/ Class is open now take heed/ it's all because of Jesus now we can breathe/ Free indeed now it's time to achieve/ as you know Jesus died for you as well as me/ Now how do we show our appreciation/ let's take a journey into revelation/ Get in accord and live by/ and always keep the lord right at your side/ Come on/

Lead III
Weak oh no, He was mighty alright/ on the third day did He not come back to life/ All false testimonies were lies/ Her proven this when He came back alive/ Oh yes, for you and me/do you not know Jesus was unique/ Trinity, the father, the son and the Holy Ghost/ and it shows/ Jesus as the logos who loves us the most/ It's okay to sing and it's okay

to rap/ God loves when we speak the truth and facts/ It's all about pleasing God in your own way/ when one is born again, everything is okay/ obey God and don't mind what others say/ for one's actions will be dealt with Judgement Day/ Come on!

I'm Pursuing It God's Way

Chorus
I'm pursuing it God's Way
I'm in this body of clay to do it the right way
Now I must say, I don't procrastinate towards my salvation, so I demonstrate.
Listen to me my brothers and sisters,
God's way is the only right way
So don't delay, Okay, Let's Pray
"Oh Heavenly Father help me to obey each and every day"

Lead I
There's a right way and wrong way on punishing things/
Now listen to the chorus and sing
Chorus
So let's obey and don't go astray from the word of our King/

Lead
Do you know what I mean, things aren't so hard as it may seem to be/ you see when you have Jesus in your life you're supposed to be striving to be pure and clean/ Oh I'm pursing God's way.

Chorus – Lead II
Life has to offer us only from what we put into it/ Now listen to my chorus sing,

Chorus
When you travel in the ways of Jesus you will benefit/ (Lead start again) Everybody comprehend, life is so beautiful when you're living right/ for you just might, gain unto the Lord, His greatest heights/ Oh I'm pursuing it God's way.

Chorus –Lead III
The way I been living wasn't working/ Now listen to my chorus sing,

Chorus
If I was pursuing in the ways of Jesus I could have been creating/ (Lead Start again) An not hurting, I recommend if you're doing things with no regard it's time to discard/ aren't you so tired,

Lead
Then wash your hands and give your life over to the care of God/

Being Inspired By God

Chorus
Being inspired by God, one may have to wait a while/ so don't whine and rest assure that He will come through on His Time/ I say being inspired by God now open your eyes/ for we are divine so let's realize to use patience as our guide/

Lead I
Being inspired by God is surely a blessing/ so take heed and believe in His Divine Lessons/ Instruction one must have to follow/ and when journey get tough don't throw in the towel/
Be consistent no matter on what it takes/ God will always be at your side so don't break/
As you know the devil would love to see us fail/ he thought he had Jesus on the cross when they nail/ Being Inspired.

Lead II
Being inspired by God when knowing our lowest patience means salvation/ come brothers and sisters and take heed to revelation/ There's time when we must learn to abide/ did not Jesus pay the way for us when He died/ He didn't have to pursue, but He knew He had to/ He paid for our sins unto Heaven we can get through/ So pay attention do you need petition/ Did I not mention, Jesus paid for our detention/ Being inspired!

Lead III
Being inspired by God, I wouldn't want it no other way/ as I Pray I then lay to obey, okay/ can't do what I want to at times/for unto the Lord I must be inspired/ For Him to lead and direct me in the toils of life/ I Know with God by my side I won't be denied/ So let's take a ride, within our state of mind/ and leave that naught and all that foolishness behind/ Being inspired!

I've Been Inspired By The Word

Chorus
I've been inspired, I cannot lie, by the word of God alone.
Oh I've been inspired, I cannot lie, by the word of God alone.
I say, I been inspired, I cannot lie by the word of God alone,
And I know when that Judgement Day comes I will be risen into His Eternal Home.

Lead I
The word of God alone has really inspired me/ you see,
I now must be about my Father's work
(Chorus) and assist those who are in need/
(Lead) Let's feed, let's eat from the word of God and do all we can/ don't pretend I recommend
(Chorus) and take It all in and comprehend/
(Lead) Let's begin, let's go, first pursing to our thoughts for that's where lies all our faults/
We need to be bold and take control from
(Chorus) From all that naught/ Oh I've been inspired!

Chorus – Lead II
The word of God alone has really set my tone/I should have known by doing things on my own/
(chorus) can only bring me harm/
(Lead) Where I belong in, His eternal Home is where I am striving to be/so unique, you see when only the word of God/
(Chorus) can get me ready for paradise that's full of felicity/
(Lead) Indeed do you agree such a place one could face/use well thy will
(Chorus) and unto God don't debase/
(Lead) When it all depends upon your actions, works and deeds/ it's worth the time to incline/
(Chorus) So you better take heed/ Oh I've been inspired

I'm A Survivor

Chorus
Oh I'm a survivor, oh yeah in Jesus name
(repeat three times)
And I'm gonna worship my God until he calls me home.

Lead I
Oh I'm a survivor in Jesus name/ and I'm not living as a lame/
Oh I'm doing all I can to not live in sin/ oh I'm representing Jesus for I can really comprehend/I say the words that Jesus speak I strive to live by/okay I pray to God to show me the way so I can be wise/ Oh I'm a survivor.

Lead II
Oh I'm a survivor in Jesus name/ For I know from whence He came/Therefore divine knowledge, wisdom, and understanding is what I strive to obtain/ I pray to God to anoint me in ways of the best/I know I need help, to enable me to defeat the negative desires of the flesh/ I confess a test that's not full of zest/but I'm a survivor in Jesus name and I know I'm blessed/

Lead III
Oh I'm a survivor in Jesus name/ I was running wild, but now I 'm sane/ I was running a race when knowing consequences as I had to race /nut when I became a survivor in Jesus name my life was no longer a waste/ I had to stop thinking I could do things all by myself/when knowing I'm a survivor in Jesus name and he's my help.

Am I worthy

Chorus
Am I worthy, I ask myself a question.
(Repeat three times)
Am I worthy to be in the presence of the Lord.

Lead I
Perfect, oh not, singing oh stop/ for in living in hell is hot/oh up and about, let's scream and shout/are you worthy then open your mouth /worthy to be in the presence of the Lord/

Lead II
Jesus died for you and me/he made us free/ oh blessed with a will to do as we please/ how are you worthy/agree I have work to do/now how about you too/ Someone who cares and always there, now ask yourself a question/Am I worthy to be in the presence of the Lord/

Lead III
The desires of our heart/so let's examine our thoughts/ Oh we need to defeat all that naught/and the negative things we were taught/ That's a good start, preparation a must, cultivation don't fuss now ask yourself a question/ Am I worthy to be in the presence of the Lord/

Letting My Spirit Direct My Flesh

Chorus
I'm letting my spirit direct my flesh (Repeat three times)/ and I 'm doing my very best. / You can do the same; You know your name/

Lead I
Being born again therefore the spirit we must revive/when knowing the flesh will one day die/Alive though still is thy spirit of God which will live on/ even more so from knowing of the blessing on why we were born/ Oh I'm letting/

Lead II
Back to the ground the flesh of dust will go one day/uphold though one's spirit which will be judge from the Lord/I must say, oh my, how are you living are you gibing into the negative desires of the flesh/ if so you need to learn how to let your spirit direct your flesh/ Oh I'm letting/

Lead III
Doing the right things in life isn't of the flesh/ it's the spirit of God within thee and He wants us to do our very best/ Such a test like no one ever manifested/that's why we need to learn how to let thy spirit direct of your flesh/ Oh I'm letting

When That Judgement Day Gonna Come

Lead – If you're not ready,
Chorus – If you're not ready
Lead – I suggest you go steady,
Chorus – I suggest you to go steady;
Lead- Because there's no telling when,
Chorus – When that judgement Day gonna come.

Lead I
Going in life, living in sin/ I tell you it's time to repent/ Aren't you tired of living a lie/ If so, it's time to become wise/ I know at times things seems so unfair/ But, God place no burden on us too much that we can't bear/ Alright now! Obedience unto God. He wants us to be/ He know we are not perfect, but He still loves you as well as me/ Now if you're not ready.

Lead II
One day at a time/ Its time out to incline/ oh thinking within your state of mind/ when it's God who should find/ Surely we must know that we can't make it on our own/ for unto God we shall always belong in Hid eternal home/ Alright now! He made it for you and for me as well/ it's all about on how we live which will determine our Heaven or Hell. / Now if you're not ready.

Lead III
Now are you ready!/If not it's time to be steady/ Let's make preparation/ It's supposed to be our obligation/ Being consistent in that which is right/ When you Know God is with You to gain the greatest heights/ Going home, on that Judgement Day it will tell/ If you're not ready, I suggest you go study before you be in hell/ Now if you are not ready.

The Spirit Of The Living God Is Upon Me

Chorus
The spirit of the living God is upon me; the spirit of the living God is upon me. In my thoughts, actions, works, deeds you are guaranteed to see; that the spirit of the living God is upon me.

Lead I
The spirit of the living God is upon me./ For I am the message that I bring, I know you all can see./ I'm a living life that is pure and very clean/ Each one teaches one, now where is the rest of my team/ The faith of God we need to propagate./ If we say we believe we shouldn't procrastinate./ Demonstrate in our thoughts, actions, works and deed.s/ As you know Jesus died for you as well as me/ The spirit.?????

Chorus –Lead II
The spirit of the living God is upon me./ One thing for sure I am not here to mislead/ So take heed I'm just trying you (to??)uplift fallen humanity/ Preparation is a must and it's my duty/ No problem at all for I was called/ I live by the word of God and His Divine Laws/ I can't fall as long as I abide/ And, out keep the Lord right be my side/ The Spirit

Chorus – Lead III
The spirit of the living God is living within side (???)/As long as I obey Him I will have eternal life/ Such a place don't you want to go to paradise/ Thrice bless up there, then down here where there must be sacrifices/ For our carnal nature could spring forth confusion/Therefore, we must not get caught up in such illusions/ Things that have never done us any good we need to get away/ As we pray to God to direct and lead us each and every day/ The spirit!

God Is Present

Chorus
God is present each and every day; therefore, we are never alone
(repeat three times)
And we need to acknowledge that He prepared for us an eternal Home.

Lead I
At times, I feel a lot of people they are so alone/ However, I'm a living witness to let you know that you are not on your own/ So whenever you feel down and out never give up your faith and hope/ Keep on praising our living God to enable you to cope/ I tell you God is present.

Chorus II
At times I know things seem not to go our way, okay let's pray/ Oh Heavenly Father, I believe in you even when it is a delay/ Say I know you know what's best therefore, I know I'm still blessed/ with that thought in mind I'm full of your zest/ I tell you God id present.

Chorus –III
At times I know things seem to be hard/ but always remember you have everything when you have God/ Such a process that you may go through/but always keep in mind that God has much love for you/ Surely, He knows what we know not/ and we should never give up on your faith like prophet Lot/ I tell you God is present

God Is My Guide

Chorus
The spirit of God is my guide (repeat three times) for it's all because of Him I'm alive. Oh when I need help/ I let the spirit of God guide my steps/ I say the spirit of God is my guide/ and I shall always abide/

Lead I
The spirit of God is my guide whenever I need guidance/ I never panic when knowing God will never leave me hanging/ Oh, I let Him lead and direct my life/ When knowing God by my side I can gain the greatest heights/ Therefore the spirit of God will always be on my eternal guide/ Oh

Chorus – Lead II
The spirit of God is my guide and I shall never mind/ Oh I may not want to rise/ but unto God I cannot denied/ And when He calls me I must obey and prepare the way/ each and every day/oh

Chorus- Lead III
The spirit of God is my guide for I know that is vey wise/ I cannot try to hide when it's time to complete the tie/ Oh it may seem as though I'm in the blind/ but I must keep in mind that God called me to shine/ The spirit of God we all need as our guide/

In The House Of The Lord

Chorus
It's nice to see you in the house of the Lord one more time/
(Repeat three times)
To worship our God who is so Divine/

Lead II
In the house of the Lord is where we belong/ Oh I love to be there to get my worship on / Cleanse my soul, oh yes be bold for it's a test/ for God wants us to be our very best/ In church we also pray/ unto Jesus who washed our sins away/
In the house of the lord.

Lead III
In the house of the Lord, I find myself always there/ Oh my God deserves all praises and I'm one who loves to share/stay home or not, get on out/fellowshipping is what it's all about/ Oh coming together in unit/ when there's so much felicity/ In the house of the Lord.

Lead III
In the house if the Lord, I also go within/ Oh I repeat and comprehend as I try not to sin/ As I help myself I can then help another/ in hopes we can come together/ For its all about God who supposed to please/ for He springs forth love and a lot of peace/ In the house of the Lord.

God Is My Light

Chorus
God is my light and this light represents the truth
(repeat three times)
And I know what in life that I need to pursue;
Now do you have a clue?

Lead I
Take heed to the word of God and obey/ If You're not ready it's time to go steady and start today/ with no delay, you may help someone along the way and God will be pleased/ some people are just too weak and you need to thank God that you are so unique to assist another who is in need/ I tell you all God is my light.

Lead –II
True indeed God wants us to shine, His light unto another/surely it's such a great pleasure when all we can come together/ Are you a member or a servant of Jesus if so that's very nice/ You can gain the greatest heights and be enlightened as long as you abide by His Divine Light/ I tell you all God is my light.

Chorus –III
God is my light and I know what I am supposed to do/how about you are living by His divine truth or is it falsehood that you choose/ You already knew why Jesus died, did He not sacrifice/ I cannot lie, one thing about God's light it shall always stay alive/ I tell you all God is my light

I Hear The Word Of God

Lead- Well I tell you brothers and sister, I hear the word of God
Chorus – So take heed and benefit
Lead- I hear the word of God
Chorus – So take heed and benefit
Lead – I hear the word of God
Chorus – So take heed and benefit, this is the way so walk in it and make a fix

Lead I
The word of God really saved me/
Unto His word I obey and show bravery/
Hey, I am just a servant of God trying to lead you to the right way/
I'm no hypocrite I am the message that I bring as you can see from my actions day by day/

Chorus – Lead II
The word of God is what we all really need/did not Jesus uplift thee by his actions, works and deeds/ take heed, for He breed unto as all so that we can live/ we can't forget from what He did so unto this cup we drink and eat of His Bread/

Chorus – Lead III
The word of God can you really hear/ if so you need to take heed and hold extremely dear/ Do you really care, do not fear, just obey every step of the way/ Let's pray, okay/ Help me oh God each and every day/ Chorus!

God's Presence In My Life

Chorus
God's presence in my life really makes a big a difference (repeat three times) and I am content as I acknowledge why Jesus was sent.

Lead
God's presence in my life really makes a big different/therefore, I do all I can when unto His word I comprehend/ actions now spring forth, as I acknowledge I must get in accord/ and I cannot ignore the word of God which can help me out for sure/God's presence in my life

Chorus – Lead II
God's presence in my life enable me to amend/ I cannot pretend as though I am perfect as I know why Jesus was sent/ Mend my faults I surely cannot do/ learning from my mistakes is all I can pursue/ God's presence in my life.

Chorus – III
God's presence in my life, makes me do right. Oh I know I can't do nothing without Him, for He is my guiding light/ I must say, "He is so wonderful in all His ways/ and God's presence in my life really brighten my days"/God's presence in my life.

The Great Divine News

Chorus
I got the great divine news that we all can use (repeat three times)/ And we need to pursue to it every day no matter on what we go through/

Lead I
The word of God is so great/ oh the word of God does create/ The word of God we need to obey/ the word of God will help us day by day/ Oh the word of God tells us not to sin/ oh the word of God/ wants us to repent/

Lead II
The word of God is so divine/ oh the word of God is so right on time/ oh the word of God can inspire/ Oh the word of God is for the weak, blind and wise/ oh the word of God calls for us to make preparation/oh the word of God is for our salvation/

Lead III
The word of God is good news/ oh the word of God is for me as well as you/ Oh the word of God it can really save/ oh the word of God is living with us today/ oh the word of God is power/ oh the word of God is for all the followers/

God Is So Worthy

Lead- Well, my brothers and sisters, I want you all to know, sing!
Chorus- God is so worthy
Lead- He put us in this body of flesh/
Chorus- God is so worthy
Lead- that's why he deserves our best/
Chorus- God is so worthy
Lead – Did not Jesus pay our penalties/
Chorus – God is so worthy
Lead- Now I am out of prosperity/
Chorus – God is so worthy
Lead – Now I am out of prosperity
Chorus – God is so worthy
Lead- Can I get a witness/
Chorus- God is so worthy
Lead – Clap your hands my Christian/
Chorus – Clap your hands like this,
Lead- If you're a Christian and witness/
Chorus- Clap your hands like this, okay Lead it's time to begin again

Lead I
You see on the cross, He wasn't lost/ He cried out tears, but He wasn't in fear/ Cared that's right for you and m/ that's why He sacrifice His Self and paid our penalties/ Worthy, indeed can you all see/ that Jesus was sent to save humanity/ We say we are this and then, we say we are that/ one thing for sure, we are nothing without God so don't lack/ Come on Chorus/ Act in the ways of Jesus/if you say you are a believer/You may at times wasn't to scream and shout/ for the Holy Ghost gave us something to roar about/

Chorus – Lead II

You see Jesus came to show the possibilities of man/for Him to do all He can as He reached out his helping hand/ Banded no one He taught human equality/the lion and the lamb when he was trying to bring about unity/You, see actions speak louder than words/Jesus teachings could have helped out Pharaoh/For everyone's soul is precious in God's sight/and it's a blessing when one allows God's good to expand in their life/come on chorus/

Destiny He wanted humanity see/belongs unto God is where we supposed to be/So unique to reach a peak which is heavenly/ I tell you brothers and sisters, God is worthy/

Jesus Is The Only Way

Chorus
Jesus is the only way, each and every day (Repeat three times)
Oh Jesus is the only way and I love pray.

Lead – I
Oh when I'm feeling down and lonely and I don't know what to do with myself/ I call on Jesus for I know he will help/ For he never lets me down even when things don't turn around right away/ I know he will come through when he is ready one day/ I say patience is a virtue that to live by/ for God that I serve is so unique and wise/ I say Jesus is the only way/

Lead II
When people try to discourage me, I always know what to do/I go to God in prayer for I know He will bring me through/ For I know the Devil is a lair and He just wants to do me wrong/ but I'm gonna lean on Jesus for my inspiration and remain strong/God is my savior and victory is assure/Jesus is the only way/

Lead III
Oh when I'm feeling weak and I don't want to do nothing at all/I know someone who is caring and loving and He answers all calls/ Don't get upset when God don't come through on your time/ Always remember God know what's best therefore there's no need to whine/ For He will always be by your side, so don't live in the blind/ I tell you all Jesus is the only way and He's always on time/

Relationship With God

I have an intimate relationship with God (Repeat three times) and I'm going to worship Him to the best of my ability, I can't forget you see

Lead I
He rescued me, you see, He transformed me/ Now I perceive on where is my destiny/ So meek, I must reach were I'm supposed to be/so much felicity when we are in tune with our divinity/Spirituality so Intune and about/ taking the word of God within and leaving falsehood out/ My relationship with God

Chorus-Lead II
He rescued me you see, now I must incline/defined the word of God and strive to live by/ For it's about that time to rise/ with the lord right at your side/so don't hide or denied on His Eternal Ride/ be wise and oblige from the goodness of the Lord that lives within side/ My relationship with God

Chorus III
He rescued me you see, now I am very pleased/ I show my appreciation for Him setting me free/I take heed to the word of God, whenever He calls/ and if I fall I get back up and obey His Divine Laws/ Flaws I must discard and when things get hard/ I can always call on my Father God/ My relationship with God.

Relationship With God
(Part II)

Chorus
Having a relationship with God is what I need (Repeat three times)/ For He will help lead and direct my life and purify my seed/

Lead I
Me and God has now a close relationship/ He created me in His image so I can benefit/ A relationship with someone who will always be there/someone who is great and who really cares/ At any second, minute, hour or day I can always call/He always listen to me and He tells me to obey His laws/

Lead II
If you need a relationship with someone, you can have it with God/ He will never let you down and He will accept you just the way you are/All he asks from us is honesty and sincerity/ and out fidelity in Him will spring forth felicity/ He wants us to change from in and out/ A close relationship with God it's what it's all about/

Lead III
Having a close relationship with God is what I strive for/Oh I know He is the only one who can save me for sure/Jesus blood for my sins made me pure/ I tell you all that the Holy Spirit is a wonderful cure/Now that I am faithful with God I feel a close connection/ I'm getting ready for that special day when I will be judged for my actions/

Lord I Just Have To Praise You

Chorus
Lord I just have to praise you (Repeat three times)
I have to praise you for giving me life and making me to be upright

Lead I
Lord unto you I have to praise/ I feel the Holy Ghost coming on and I am amazed/ At timed I scream and may even shout/ for I know what the emotion is all about/ Lord I don't know the time nor the day/ So in the meantime I'm going to be pleasing you before you take me away/come on help me!

Lead II
Lord you gave me life and I am pleased/ One of the ways I show my thanks when I pray on my knees/I say Lord you been good to me/ I know you are all good and I'm going to do my very best/ come on help me!

Lead III
Lord you are forever on my mind/you gave me life and I'm going to utilize my time/ I know without you, I'm nothing/you created me out of dust and made me into something/ I know you are coming for me one day that's why I am so steady/ I will have a smile on my face from knowing I am ready/ Come on help me!

For Us Jesus Gave His Life

Chorus
For Jesus gave His life/He wanted us to be upright/Such a task that we need to pursue/since the trials and tribulations that he been through/It's something we should want to do/reassure Him that we love Him too/

Lead I
The punishment we deserve, Jesus tool upon himself/when he died on the cross he didn't even cry out for help/For he already knew what he was called to do/ he done all he done out of love for me as well as you/He bared our sins on the cross/ He wanted us to have hope and faith for he knew we was lost/Jesus gave his life.

Lead II
The punishment we deserve; Jesus took all the blame/We need to show our appreciation to Him from why he came/He died for you as well for me/bless was the third day when he arose from the deep/sleep not for too long for he knew where he belongs/For he is a mighty God who never done any wrong/Jesus gave his life.

Lead III
The punishment we deserve Jesus bared our sins away/he lets us know there's more to life than this body of clay/He say, there's another place that we have to face/and Jesus wants us to prepare for it each and every day/Hey say, another place is hell and I know you don't want to go there/always keeping in mind Jesus died for us because he really cares/

It Is The Holy Spirt

Chorus
It is the Holy Spirit that brings about a transformation/ come brothers and sisters it's time to make a preparation. / This isn't a joke, can you cope, if so then grab your spiritual coat and let's go and grow.

Lead I
The Holy spirit indeed it can bring about a change/the will of God is powerful now can you obtain/the will of God now working in you/trials and tribulation that we all must go through/Remaining strong when knowing where you belong as we build for the future and our eternal home/There's work now that we need to pursue/so don't refuse what's on the menu/If you choose to disobey/ the wrath of God will come down on you one day/Let's thank Jesus who bared our sins away/

Lead II
The Holy Spirit gives power to get on a mission/it's my tradition/but first I had better my conditions/I'm living in the world, but not to be caught up in it/ I take heed to the word of God and benefit/ If I slip and fall I get right back up/repent from my sins even when the roads get tough/Such a learning experience which I take heed/repeat the same sins oh no, I defeat/ Bringing in my will in tune with the will of God/Keeping prayer alive when knowing things will get hard/Guards up at all times, as I use my mind/for me to incline, I first had to define/

Lead III
The Holy spirit all I can say it's so unique/Trinity one, two, three now can we keep/ Living within thee I can't denied/we need to realize God hated when we tell a lie/Straight up we need to face our mistakes/if you have the Holy Spirit you will love instead of hate/Holy Ghost up in smoke now we can cope/God loves when we keep our faith and hope/The Holy Spirit right now is living within thee/All praised is due to Jesus who came to set us free in deed/

Love One Another

Chorus
There is action we need to take and that is love one another (Repeat three times)/in sight of God we all are one so let's love together?

Lead I
God so love the world that He sent His only begotten son/He didn't have to do such but He did, now let's have a lot of fun/In loving one another If you haven't started then get on the shore/and make joyful noise and come abroad/and be the best we can be/and stay in tune with our spirituality/

Lead II
God loves us so much more when we really love another/obeying Him is what brings Him pleasure/Such a test in the flesh now do you protest to be at your best/I confess I love is the savior of the world and Jesus did manifested/And He said what I can do we all can now when are we gonna begin/let's first start to conquer our sins and repent/

Lead III
God is that only one we supposed to please/ and we do such by loving on another now do you really agree/ Freeze at ease now when actions speaks louder than words haven't you heard/such a divine love that lives within you as well as me/ loving on another brings about peace/

The Devil Is Liar

Chorus
The Devil is a liar and he has no saving power (Repeat three times) and He always seeking followers so keep your faith in the Lord, and unto the devil don't bow.

Lead I
The devil is a liar do you all really know/ Let's go, for within our thoughts we need to gain some self-control/

Chorus –Lead II
The devil can only gain His strength by us giving to him/
Chorus – So don't give in.
Lead – Don't let Him win He only represent when we living in sins/
I recommend our defeat our negative thoughts which lies our faults
And take heed to what Jesus taught/Caught up in naught to hark/
Oh, the Devil is a liar/

Chorus – Lead II
The Devil can only gain His Strength by us giving to him/
Chorus – So don't give in
Lead – Don't let Him win He only can represent when we are living in sins
I recommended our defeat our negative thoughts which lies our faults
And take heed to what Jesus taught/Caught Up in naught to hark/
Oh, the Devil is a liar/

Chorus – Lead III
The Devil is a liar and I refuse to allow Him to bring me pain/
Chorus – He is insane/
Lead- I obtain all goodness from God therefore, I must always use my brain/

Chorus-So let's train/

Lead-Not in vain, it's time to gain when knowing God created us not to be lame/the devil is

Liar who is up to know good with his foolishness games/ oh the devil is a liar!

One Day I Will Be Going Home

Chorus
One day I will be going home to be with my Lord
To be with my Lord
I don't know when it's going to be
I don't know when it's going to be
But I know I will be ready
Oh yes indeed!

Lead I
No one knows the time nor day/ so I pray unto God that I will always obey/ Okay let's stay with the word of God and Abide/ And don't hide nor deny why on the cross which Jesus died/Lied as they crucify, they even tried to boast/and on the third day they were surprised when He arose/So let's go, one day.

Lead II
Any second, minute or hour when God holds the power/come brothers and sisters we need that divine knowledge/when knowing wisdom is that knowledge being applied/so we need to build for our eternal future so when the flesh dies/Revive and arise to a new plane/ a new heart, mind and soul which we must obtain/so let's go, one day

Lead III
Do you know if you're going to heaven or hell/how are you living, surly your actions will tell/You may say this and that but is it fact/one thing for sure God knows of things that we lack/So watch your back on the things you say/for we reap what we sow and it will show on that Judgement Day/So let's go, one day!

If You Are Grieving

Chorus

If you are grieving you need to shout it on out, (No doubt)
If you are grieving, you need to shout it on out (And be up and about)
If You are grieving, you need to shout it on out (Oh Yeah!)
And don't be too slow and let God take control, for it's time to grow, so let's go.

Lead I

Surely, God knows whatever you're going through/ (I thought you knew)
Don't you know what God is right by your side, so let Him Pursue/ (Do you need a clue)
For God place no burden on us too much that we can't bare/ (Now that's fair) for He is Just and loving God who really cares/ If You are grieving.

Chorus – Lead II

It's time to wake up for you been grieving too long/ (take heed to this song)
I know you lost your love one but God want you to be strong/ (Sound the alarm)
I know at times it's not too easy (I agree) and that's when you need to call on Jesus to help you relieve/ If you are grieving.

Chorus – Lead III

We have people grieving each and every day/ (Okay) now when are we gonna let go and let God have His way/ (Let's Pray) Oh God I know you can hear me so I'm asking you to help me/ (Over this pack) for I'm stress out and very weak. So please help your sheep/ Oh I'm grieving!

The Creation

Chorus

It was the creation and the fall of man/ Some people out there needs to understand/ That it was the Holy breath blown into man/ For him to strive and to do all he can/ such as to overcome his negative folds/ on the physical plane he needs to gain some self-control/ That hope will be his beacon light/ When knowing there's numerous foes and obstacles that we must be fight/ To be the strength of God that we must manifest/ we strive and toil to be our very best/

Chorus

It is the Holy breath, blown into man/ It is the Holy breath for Him to strive and do all he can/ It is the Holy Breath, yes we now have life/ It is the Holy Breath, to enable us to gain the greatest heights/

Lead II

I'm here to build a nation, it's call for cultivation/ when preparation is along the way towards my destination/ procrastination oh no, for I'm always on top/ I put the work into it to reach my ultimate goal/ If you can see it then believe you can achieve / Put forth the efforts and most likely you will breed/ Agree humanity we are free/ To do as we want bless with a will indeed/ Need a plan to advance give yourself and you enhance/ His wonderful creation He has made/ We need to give all praises to Him each and every day/ Say, raise your hands in the air/ Oh, yeah, show your gratitude for the father who cares/ Let's share, such a love that's so divine/ do you mind God didn't leave us in the blind/ So let's find a way to bring about unity/ You see we need to get in tune with is divinity/ That's unique, hard at time but we must define/ God's sign are very beneficial to us incline/ That's wise now we can't really denied/ don't lie, growth and development must start within side/ Oh my, we can't really hide/ for the reality of situation is still alive/ Abide, it's time to really rise/ let's shine, come humanity let's complete the tie/

Being At Peace

Chorus
Serenity now listen to me/ for I'm here to please and bring about peace/ So freeze let's bring things at ease/ everybody I'm gonna set y'all souls free/ so listen up, listen up, humanity/ you agree God wants us to live in Felicity/

Lead I
Oh my, where shall I go, where shall I start/ let's purse to our sins that we need to depart/ Free indeed, now let's flow and grow you know/ when foes and obstacles are in the way we have to let go/ On the first step we find it's belief/ on the next step is faith and we must toil, to keep/ Fruition that's right now I'm on divine a mission/ all praises are due to God for my right decisions/ Trying to build a nation, its call for preparation/ come brother and sisters it's a call for cultivation/ Transformation, oh yes, now let us pray/ Meditation when He speak to us to listen up and obey/ observation, interpretation and application/ when all praises is due to God for revelation/ Being at peace!

Lead II
Oh my, where shall I go, where shall I start/ Let's flow in our minds where our sins lie in our thoughts/ Take heed and believe that we can achieve/ when God comes first now here comes prosperity / Fidelity in God we must keep indeed/ only the master of creation will know His sheep/sleep oh no, I must uphold/grow and unfold to make my nobility show/ God, oh yes, I must shine/ and represent God who is so divine/ Blind once but know I see/ as I thank Jesus for dying for you and me. Unique when no other ways of His kind/ Jesus came to revive our hearts and minds/ Being at peace!

Lead III

Oh my, where shall I go, where shall I start/if we going to live in peace then we must defeat that naught/ Thought a lot of things that we are disgrace/ when we reap what we sow then we have to face/Grace of Jesus when He died on the cross/he done it out of mercy and love for we were lost/ Toss all our negativity and sins out the door/ as we take heed why Jesus came aboard/ I ignore oh no we cannot do/ when knowing Jesus died for me and you/ pursue on the menu from what he went through/ now which type of actions are you gonna choose/ Misuse oh no, don't be a fool/when knowing Jesus came to put out Satan's fuse/

I'm Gonna Fight This War With Jesus

Chorus
I'm gonna fight this war with Jesus (Repeat three times) For He is worth fighting gore.

Lead I
I'm gonna fight this war with Jesus until the day I die/ and I know there's s something within me that will revive/ When kneeing there's a journey within me that I need to fight for, I'm for sure the Holy Spirt will lead me through the right door/Oh I'm gonna fight this war.

Lead II
I'm gonna fight this war since God is for me/ Foes and obstacles may be in my way but God will help me please/ I can't defeat this war without Him at times I pray on my knees/

Lead III
I'm gonna fight this war no matter whatever it takes/for I'm living for God, I shall not procrastinate/ I'm on a journey when knowing I'm not fighting this war alone/ and I shall not rest until I reach my eternal home/

Jesus Died On The Cross

Chorus
Jesus died on the cross when He really didn't have to/but He died for He was called to bring his people through/ Now we suppose to appreciate Him in every way/ If you haven't you need to start today/
Lead I
Oh I found my way, when I was lost/ I went to Jesus and acknowledge why He died on the cross/ I know I had to repent from my sinful ways/for eternal nature it's something I have to fight each and every day/ Jesus died on the cross/
Lead II
Now that I found my way, I will try to do my very best/ As I acknowledge, every step of the way, the devil will try to detest/ Here's my faith now and I know I must remain strong/for I know in God is where I belong/ Oh Jesus died on the cross/
Lead III
Now sin lies in our thoughts and we must try to depart/ and purify our hearts with the love of God is a good start/ And we must be forever mindful that the devil will try to remain/therefore we must stay on guard and use our brains/ Jesus stay on guard and use our brains/ Jesus died on the cross/

I'm Letting God Have His Way

Chorus
I'm letting God have his way (Repeat three times)
Each and every day, it's okay to pray.

Lead I
Day by day, I pray now I must say/ I have to let God have His way before it be too late/ Decay, I don't know when it's going to be/ but I know my spirit will rise and I will be ready/ You see there's more to life than what it seems/ therefore, more to life than what it seems/therefore, I strive and toil to be purify and clean/ How can I really let God have His way/ I must obey His law each and every day/ Now I'm letting!

Lead II
My, My, My, I must incline/so I'm letting God have His way before I run out of time/So divine, when I'm striving and toiling to get in accord/ when knowing unto God I consider not to ignore/purity unto my soul is what I'm working for/in my actions, works and deeds I always take a tour/cure is what I really need/ that's when I pray, oh lord, help me please/ Now I'm letting!

Lead III
When letting God have His way it is truly a blessing/even more so when one obeys His divine lessons/Testing is something God takes us through/ and when letting God have His way, you will know what to pursue/such a clue you know when things seem to go wrong/ and we turn to God who is mighty strong/ In hopes He will take our problems and work them out/from the devil who seems to be up and about/

Too Much Of Me

Chorus

Oh, too much of me is in the world, oh too much of me is of the flesh, too much of me that I need to protest, I confess, we need to be our very best. We need to start today!

Lead I

Living in this world is not easy/but we can be free when living for Jesus/Chasing in the world of illusions/ do you not know that it only brings about confusion/ A change of the flesh to astray/ all tempting thoughts that are naught that we need to get a way/ that are naught that we need to stop/sinning is that we need to stop/ as we acknowledge, God is the only one who is on top/

Lead II

A lifetime change, we need to start today/ for living after the flash is something we need to decay/ Hey obey God for the truth will set us free/ don't you agree indeed that the carnal nature is weak/ Keep oh no, let go and take control/ For God really love us don't you know/ We need to start today.

Lead III

A change of mind it's about that time/ We don't suppose to love after the flesh for we are so divine/ And God wants us to live a life that's pure/ He already know we are not perfect; however, He brought us a cure/ Now it's all up to us to get on board/for Jesus already gave us the tour/ We need to start today.

I Put On The New Me

Chorus

I took off my old self and put on the new (Repeat Three times) oh yeah, for there are trials and tribulations that we all must go through/

Lead I

Transformation in indeed, say oh Lord please/ cultivation oh Lord I'm still in need/ Oh help me defeat and beat/ the things in life that are weak/ A new way of living s what I am striving for/ I'm developing a Christ like character that's so unique and pure/. Oh I took off my old self.

Lead II

Being born again a better life a new/when our old ways we need to subdue/ I revive don't you hide when you can't be denied/ the reality inside that's still alive/Oh you may stumble and fall but know you can always call/ On God for He is near and not far/ Oh I took off my old self/

Lead III

Inspiration in deed, say old Lord please/preparation, Oh Lord, I'm in need/ Oh Lost at times when there's nowhere to go/Oh Lord I pray for self-Control/ Unfold and grow when I must be bold/when knowing God place no burden on us too much that we can't hold!

Christen Have Made Us Free

Chorus
Christ have made us free, don't you all agree/ Oh Christ have made us free, don't you all agree; I say Christ have made us free. He died so we could reach heaven you see/

Lead I
Christ has done for us like no one else/when we are in trouble who do we call out for help/ Jesus I love to call His name/For He's so unique now do you know why He came/ Inspired do you know why in hope to rise us beyond the sky/ Wise oh yes He is Mighty Great/ He's like no other and He came to save/ Sins He paid the way and took our Load/behold, He was bold when He rose/Uphold He unfolded on Calvary/when He died for you as well as me/I tell you Christ have made!

Lead II
Christ was He not mighty strong/ I hope you take heed to His Mighty song/ We need to prepare for Our eternal home/ When knowing no, one knows how far and long/ When knowing preparation that's right is the key/to get where we are going for eternity/Unique in deed now don't you want to go/ it's like nothing on earth haven't you been told/Gold when you van benefit/ A lifetime here can't be compared/ with the after their life now did you past or fail/ I tell you Christ have made!

Lead III
Jesus was surely one of a kind/ did He not do mighty miracles such as healed the blind/ For those with eyes did see indeed/ How wonderful God was when He help those in need/ He even forgave those who done Him Wrong/ When knowing He had the power to bring them harm/ But He knew of His creation and condition/ So He didn't fall from His divine mission/ He could have started a lot of confusion/ but He knew everything and the illusions/I tell you Christ have made!

I Surrender Unto You Lord

Chorus

I surrender unto you Lord, for I know you are in control (Repeat three times) I can't do nothing without you God, so please bless my soul/

Lead I

Going through life now who is in control/you may have to rethink, for its God who runs the show/ You may think you bold, well you been told/you been serve now you already know/ You may have to reconsider and surrender/unto God and always remember/ That He has the final say so/when knowing He supposed to be our ULTIMATE GOAL/Now which way to go, do we need to unfold/when knowing it's God who is in control/I surrender!

Lead II

When you surrender unto God you need to give all/when you don't have anyone who can you always call/Unto God who will never leave/unto God who is never asleep/ Keep your negative ways oh no, it's time to stop/when knowing it's God who is at the very top/For the power I have I can't pursue it alone, it is of God's doing and He's set the tone/ I surrender!

Lead III

I surrender unto God and it's for the best/ I must confess I'm building for my eternal nest/ I can't do nothing on my own/when knowing unto God. I belong/ Gave me a will to choose from as I use my mind/I surrender my all as I defend/I yield to the power of God/ I obey and follow His laws/ And when things are hard and I can't obtain/ I pray unto God from whence I came/I surrender!

The Divine Love Of God

Lead I
The divine love of God we need to demonstrate/we should procrastinate tomorrow what we can pursue today. We say we love but our actions don't show/we say we love but our actions don't show/we say we love each other then we don't uphold/ Let go, oh no, did God leave us alone/ He always been there for us now let's pick up the spiritual phone/ Hello Father, I know you are there/You sent Jesus to us to let us know you really care/ Help me Lord to show, my love to another/protect us Lord to always stay together/ I know Lord conditions does change/ So please Lord let the divine love remain/

Chorus
The divine love of God is still living (Repeat three times) and we shouldn't procrastinate but demonstrate and start giving/

Lead II
The divine love of God we need to show in our actions, works and deeds/ Oh Lord, help me please/ I know I am not worthy/ Agree indeed but I still have a job to pursue/even more so from knowing all Jesus went through/ We say we love but then our actions tells us else/ I think we need help and a lot of people are caught up on self/ Rearrange when it's time to obtain/The Divine Love of God from whence we came/

Lead III
The divine love of God is living within/it helps to repent from sin to be able to represent/We say we love but out actions doesn't match/ We say we this and that but then we lack/Such a fact we can't deny from being blind/When it's God that we need who is so divine/When you think you have it all figured out/ your actions will tell and not from what comes of your mouth/

God Commanded Us To Pray

I say we pray because God commanded us to pray (Repeat Three times) if you're not committed you need to start today!

Lead I
If you need a change in your life/oh pray to God and He will make you alright/Just keep your faith along the way/ and pray to God each and every day/Keep your head up and always obey/ the word of God and What He has to say/ Let's pray, Oh God, give me strength, so I can become strong/ to fight foes and obstacles that bring me harm/For the devil is always up and about/ and I'm going to keep praying to God to keep the devil out/Come, oh help me!

Lead II
When we pray, we need to be sincere/when we share we must realize God does care/Always there when we really need/ On my knees Oh Lord help me please keeping it real and done dare conceal/praying to God when you eat your meal/He knows how you feel and what you are going through/ups and downs is part of life that we must pursue/Let's pray Oh God, I can't do thus all by myself/I come to you Heavenly father for I know you can help/Oh God, I know the Devil is a liar/that's why you as my spiritual guide/come on help me!

Lead III
I'm on the right path with no delay/Unto God I always pray/He's the only one who gets my all/and when I fall I know He Will hear my call/ I shall keep, my faith and hope/He place no burden too much that I can't cope/ Let's pray, Oh God, keep me spiritual awake/ teach me how to love instead hate/ Oh God you have my best interest at heart/and I will take heed to Luke 11:1, when Jesus taught/Come on help me!

Get Up And Praise The Lord

Chorus
Get up and praise the Lord if you're not doing it enough, you need to pursue some more/Come on help me!

Lead I
If you're lacking then you need to become steadfast/and raise the Lord praise like it's no tomorrow before you past/That's right you need to give God all the praise you got/and watch out for the Devil who is always up and about/Stop and defeat and praise the devil out/get on up and praise the Lord, it's okay to shout/Oh praise the Lord at all times/For He is worthy do we need to define/Blind, oh no, we have our self-control/eyes to use do you need to be told/uphold blessed with another day/say there's more to life than this body of clay/ Come on help me!

Chorus – Lead II
Praise the Lord even when things get rough/and keep your faith in Him and never fuss/ For He will come through one day/so keep praising Him along the way/Delay someone might just go through/ but that doesn't mean He doesn't hear you/ He's always there/and you can rest assure that He really cares/a lot of people get upset I must say/when things doesn't turn out their way/Looking for someone to blame/when you need to look within and obtain/View at your action what you're pursuing today/ now do you know the things you need to deviate/Get away for its time to be strong/when knowing there's a lot to be thankful for/ for instance let's take a little tour/Ears to hear when God we fear/ eyes to see now that's unique /Hands to feel, didn't Jesus healed blessed with a mind comprehend/when knowing we can do all things, come on girls, boys, woman, and men/

Faith With Works

Chorus
Faith without works is dead, just as a body with no spirit is dead (Repeat three times)
Now what are we going to do? I can't hear you, what works are you going to pursue/alright now. Don't forget Jesus died for me as well as you too/

Lead I
We say we have faith if so did your actions spring/ Oh we know faith without works is dead so what did you bring/ In the record of the Lord, He did record/ our actions, works, and deeds He will know if we ignore/ Faith with works

Lead II
Faith with works is dead now, what is going on in your head? /oh do you really care on the blood if Jesus that He shed / You say you do but your actions say something else/ We must always be forever mindful that we are living for God and not for ourselves/some need to put forth efforts that let God know that we really have faith/ and one way to show Him is to love instead of hate/oh, we need faith with works/

Lead III
Faith with works supposed to be forever/ God loves when we work together/It's not of me but of God who we supposed to be happy/Feeling good at times for all of your good deeds/ actions speak louder than words now where is your fidelity/Integrity living inside thee, now whose really free. /faith with works is something we need indeed/

We Can't Have It Both Ways

Chorus

We can't serve two Gods at one time. I must say, we need to pray
(Repeat three times)
We can't have it both ways, some need to make that decision today/

Lead I

There's a right way of doing things and a wrong way also/so we need to
take control and choose which way to go/knowing at times we may get
weak but we must be determined to defeat/as we keep in mind on Jesus
who was so unique/

Lead II

There are material things people tend to serve more than their God/and
I tell you all you have to let go no matter how it seems to be hard/You
either hate one and love the other, now what's your real pleasure / I tell
you God is the first/ and only one, who spring forth an eternal treasure/

Lead III

There are things in life that seem to bring us harm/we can't have it both
ways so do what's tight and you will remain strong/Do away with sin
and repent and you shall always be glad/we have the good and evil and
the happy and mad/

The Real Deal

Chorus
The Real deal
Someone who has the capacity to heal
The Real deal someone who is so genuine so real
The Real deal
Someone who really cares
The Real deal
Someone who loves to share

Lead I
The real deal
One who is living for God
Concerns of the people, as one obeys His divine laws
The Real Deal
Needs of the other one is always there
Oh How He feels one surely bares
The real deal
Purpose in life unto God one does please
To the upmost one pursues to be at ease
The Real deal
Keys when knowing who's the best holder
Unto God, when knowing He's the Real Best Molder
The Real Deal
Older doesn't mean you are the best
Actions, words, and deeds do matter what you manifest

Lead II
The Real Deal
One who is committed
Living for God as one stays on mission
The Real deal

Nothing at all getting in one's way
Living in the world but not if it today????
The Real deal
Say, one who has ultimate goal
Told when Jesus already paid our toll

The Real deal
So let one really be strong
Such an obligation unto God to bring no harm
The Real Deal
Belongs unto Him forever
Are you the Real deal trying to uplift others?
Lead III
The Real Deal
One who is living by the word
Haven't you heard one doesn't supposed to be of the world
The Real deal
One who would never kill
Always living in accordance with God's will
The Real Deal
No Joke, one living in faith and hope
Cope, oh yeah, whenever inspired with the Holy Ghost
The Real deal
Let's go, you know on how you supposed to be
See when God created us all so unique
The Real Deal
In deed when He supply all our needs
Whenever we are in trouble we say "Oh Lord, Help me please"

www.ingramcontent.com/pod-product-compliance
Lightning Source LLC
Chambersburg PA
CBHW021349090426
42742CB00008B/795